The Swamps

Ekpe Inyang

Langaa Research & Publishing CIG
Mankon, Bamenda

Publisher:
Langaa RPCIG
Langaa Research & Publishing Common Initiative Group
P.O. Box 902 Mankon
Bamenda
North West Region
Cameroon
Langaagrp@gmail.com
www.langaa-rpcig.net

Distributed in and outside N. America by African Books Collective
orders@africanbookscollective.com
www.africanbookscollective.com

ISBN: 9956-762-38-5

DISCLAIMER
All views expressed in this publication are those of the author and
do not necessarily reflect the views of Langaa RPCIG.

Foreword

The Swamps presents a debauched tapestry of the utterly dehumanised society in which Ekpe Inyang shows a community to have degenerated since his dramaturgy aims at a controlled and comprehended synthesis of human awareness. There is a judicious deployment of myth, history as well as parables, song, mimicry and dance. The inclusion of these features of orature in this political allegory creates not only particular moods and atmospheres but lends colour and movement to dramatic action.

The structure and function of *The Swamps* defines the individual's identity within the cosmic context which approximates the past and present. In the play in which ritual and secret cults play a functional role within the community the audience is confronted with a multi-dimensional experimentation in subject matter and form.

Mytho-poetic intent shows character types in all their finite ramifications and dialectical contradictions. These are seen in the forces which embody the irreconcilable goals of classes within the society. The playwright's analysis of class political behaviour in Obon Obini's Ekon exposes the complete erosion of civil liberties by corrupt and venal elite who have usurped political and economic power by virtue of their inheritance of the state apparatus. The element of instability is reflected in the fragility of political institutions characterized by violence and marked by an absence of commitment to the national ethos.

This playwright has impressed the theatre audience with his dramatic eloquence and the fervour of his commitment, and emblazoned his name in the front ranks of the alternative theatre in Cameroon. For, as a cultural cartographer, Ekpe Inyang confronts the hot button issues of contemporary reality thereby validating the axiom that the writer's task is one which entails a sensibility that would be used to express a vision that is relevant in time.

A rare theatrical gem...demonstrates a brilliant, sustained invention...greater depth and suggestive power...

Bate Besong, PhD
Department of English
University of Buea, Cameroon

Characters in the Play

OBON OBINI, *the king of EKON*
OSERE *highest members*
AKPARIKA *of the Royal Council*
1ST MESSENGER *the Royal*
2ND MESSENGER *messengers*
MORUWA, *praise-singer / clan crier*
KATAI, *an elite of Ekon*
OROKA, *his wife*
SOKORO, *another elite and friend of KATAI*
KENWENG, *the most powerful wrestler in Ekon*
ALL, *clan crowd, including the king's*
BODYGUARDS and DRUMMERS
VOICE, *a mystery voice*
1ST VOICE *voices from*
2ND VOICE *the clan crowd*
A FIGURE *eavesdropping*
BAKANI, *ancestral spirits*

[Early morning. The veranda of KATAI's house. KATAI is sitting in an old arm chair, cleaning his teeth with a chewing stick. OROKA, a young woman of about twenty-two, emerges from the house. She carries a wash-hand basin in both hands, a small towel flung over her left shoulder. She bangs the basin down angrily on the floor in front of KATAI and deposits the towel on KATAI's lap. Then she makes a sudden and dramatic turn back into the house.]

KATAI: What's all this nonsense? It were better
    You didn't bring me the water, rather than set
    A basket of trouble at my feet this early morning.

OROKA *[Appears at the door, standing arms akimbo,*
and looks back with a sneer.]: You think that if I didn't eat
    I'd have the strength and energy to sweep the
    House, fetch water, wash the plates, search for
    Firewood, cook the food...?

KATAI: Hold it! Too early for all that. Indeed.
    You may come and take your water away,
    Rather than stand there and spit
    All you can on me. *[OROKA disappears into the*
    house.] Is this all it means to be married?
    Talk, talk, talk everyday? When shall I ever have
    Peace in this house? I'm tired of it all,
    Really tired and sick of it.

[He starts to wash his face. Enter SOKORO rather stealthily.]

SOKORO: Good morning, da Katai.

KATAI [*Looks up, startled.*]: Oh it's you, da Sokoro?
  Good morning. What's up? Why so early today?

SOKORO [*Ignoring the questions.*]: You are lucky
  To have a wife who gives you water to wash your face
  In the morning, da Katai.

KATAI: Indeed? I wish you were here to witness the
  drama.
  She nearly threw the water onto my feet.

SOKORO: That shouldn't surprise me. You certainly
  Did not handle her well last night.
  Maybe you took too much ofofo.

KATAI [*Jokingly.*]: Come on! I know you'll never lack
  A new way of teasing me. Perhaps I should tell you
  How much I suffer these days.

SOKORO: No! Top secret!

KATAI: Can you imagine it? All because
  I don't give her enough money to take
  To the market nowadays.

SOKORO [*Teasingly.*]: And why don't you, da Katai?
  I hope you are not inviting me again to act as a judge.

KATAI [*A little bit embarrassed.*]: Oh, well!
  I guess you must be kidding again.

SOKORO: Yes, I am. Do I need to tell you
  What our women are? To them a man is a brook

That knows not dry season.
Mention the word crisis, and they'll tell you
It's a slogan used by men so they could shirk
Their responsibility without blame.
But, I think, it won't take long before they learn
And become cooperative.

KATAI: Cooperative? Did you say cooperative?
[*Resumes washing his face.*] Well...you certainly
   Know what you mean cooperative.
   A woman, my father once told me...

SOKORO: That's being conservative, da Katai.
   Most women do cooperate with their men
   These days.

KATAI [*Still washing his face.*]: In other tribes, perhaps.

SOKORO: Here in our tribe. Even in this very clan.
   I can cite you a few examples. Do you know,
   For instance, why da Ojom succeeded in
   Building his house? It was because his wife
   cooperated...

KATAI [*Sarcastically, completing the sentence for
SOKORO.*]: In bringing forth many children
   And many problems.

SOKORO: You will never understand?

KATAI: I need not tell you what our mate
   Is going through.

SOKORO: Going through what?

KATAI: Don't you see what he looks like?
    No one would ever believe that
    This is a man who once carried
    A stomach that danced like a sack of cotton. *[SOKORO*
    laughs rather unconsciously.]
    Oh! Don't laugh. The man is not himself again.
    Too much thinking: thinking how to keep
    His family going, thinking how to pay his debt.
    You know he borrowed money from the clan Njangi
    In order to complete his housework?
    Now he can't pay back the money.
    His gun has failed him;
    His farm is fast becoming a thick bush:
    No money to pay workers to do the clearing.
    All this is now reflected on his very look.
    The muscles, as if the bones
    On which they lie were ovens, get burnt
    And dried up everyday.
    He will soon get drained dry of the sap of life,
    And become nothing but an empty shell.
    In fact, our women are terrible.
    See what they can do to a man?

SOKORO: So you blame the women, eh?

KATAI: Yes. Or do you know a man who
    Deserves a dose of blame in
    This matter? *[A pause.]* Ask one of the women
    To stop giving birth after, say,
    The third child and you'll know what
    I'm talking about. They do not care,

Let alone appreciate the difficulty
  A man encounters
  Just to keep the family breathing.

SOKORO: Well, I have a strong conviction:
    The women will soon face it, and then they will learn.
    Even a little child knows that today
    Times are hard. Crises knock at every door.
    Except, perhaps, at the doors of those
    Specialised in siphoning….

KATAI: Wait a minute.

SOKORO: I'm sorry, that's not what has
    Brought me here so early.
    We have something far more crucial to discuss.
    Remember what we talked about the other day?
    We need to discuss the issue at length.

*[KATAI wipes his face with the small towel, places the
basin at a corner and hangs the towel on a line at the
veranda. SOKORO observes him keenly and eagerly.]*

KATAI: Yes, da Sokoro? What did we talk about?
    We've been discussing many, many subjects, you know:
    Women, politics, school life. Which, precisely,
    Do you mean now?

SOKORO: Leadership. This thorny issue of
    Leadership...in this clan of ours.

KATAI: Oh, yes. I remember well.
SOKORO: Many murmur, but no one is bold enough

To come out openly and question it.
It is time we lifted our fingers and
Raised our voices
To express our bitter resentment against
The irregularities in the system.

KATAI: You are right, da Sokoro.
We cannot afford to keep quiet now.
Our parents kept quiet, and see
What is happening today.

SOKORO: Now we have a system
That every sane mind would loathe.
A system that a God-fearing soul would
Stand up against. A system that any patriotic
Citizen would strive to destroy. A system that...

KATAI: Hold your peace, da. We must not turn
The whole arrangement into an anthem
To be sung so loud that the birds of the air
Soon pick up the tune and sing it to every clan
And clime. Let us plan our strategy...quietly.
But before we do this, I have two pertinent
Questions that we must answer.
Let none of us be defensive.

SOKORO [*With an air of confidence.*]: Go ahead.

KATAI: Good. First, I want us to consider
What we can realistically do
To address this leadership problem.

SOKORO: Easy affair! Don't you…?

KATAI: Hold on for a moment. That was
    My first question; and the second one is
    Whom are we going to involve,
    If there is anything at all we can do? *[Emphatically.]*
    Let's consider these questions carefully
    And rationally.

SOKORO *[Immediately.]:* Thank you very much.
    It's all simple. We must destroy the system.
     Completely.

KATAI: How? It's not enough to say
    We must destroy the system;
    Just how do we do it?

SOKORO *[Getting emotional.]:* Da Katai, Don't you try to...
    I mean this is not a joking matter.

KATAI: I'm not joking, da Sokoro.
    Keep your emotions at bay. *[A short pause.]*
    We need to come out with something concrete
    And realistic. Planning involves
    A lot of thinking and rethinking, you know.
    You just can't jump out of bed, with your eyes
    Still cloudy with sleep, and...Well, this, as you've noted,
    Is a really crucial issue.
    And we need to come out with a realistic plan of
     action.

SOKORO: There is a way out *[...]* Yes. All I want us to
    do,
    At this juncture, is agree on destroying the system.

How to go about it will be worked out later.

KATAI: [Sceptically.]: Worked out later?

SOKORO [Angrily.]: Wait a minute! Are you insinuating
that
We do not have enough courage and determination
To destroy this despotic system?

KATAI: Of course not, we have already agreed
To destroy the system. By the simple fact that we do
Appreciate that it is bad. Now another question.
Who do we involve? Because, you will agree with me,
Just the two of us cannot do anything. Well, we can,
In a sense, but...We need supporters. Or don't you
Think so, da Sokoro?.

[A FIGURE tip-toes in and hides behind the right side wall.]

SOKORO [With airs.]: Many are behind us.
They know that we are all exploited. Oppressed.
Marginalised. In fact, they are sick and tired
Of this despotic system and are prepared
To give their unflinching support
To any movement that aims to crush it into dust.

KATAI [Logically.]: Name me one.

SOKORO: You doubt what I am saying, da Katai?
Or do you link the effort with a vain experiment?

KATAI: No. But I simply want to know the crop of
people
We hope to involve.

SOKORO: Kenweng is one of them.

KATAI: Hmm...I have my doubts.

SOKORO: Why?

KATAI *[Cynically.]*: Kenweng is a strong
    And powerful man,
    This is undoubted. But *[...]* I'm afraid,
    He is a coward.

SOKORO: What did you say?

KATAI *[Bluntly.]*: Kenweng is a coward.
    You may not believe this. *[Brief silence.]*
    By the way, have you talked to him about the issue yet?
    Do talk to him and see if he's willing and prepared
    To take such a risk *[…]* Yes, it is a risk.

SOKORO *[Confidently.]*: He will, he must.

KATAI: You can't make such a wild assumption, da
    Sokoro.
    Nor should you make it sound like an imposition.
    It has to come out of one's volition, you know.
    Not like conscripting men to fight a war
    Whose meaning and cause they do not understand.

SOKORO: I will talk to him.

KATAI: Yes. You need to talk to him first,
    And it is up to him to decide whether or not

To support the cause. You can't force it on him, can
    you?

SOKORO: Well…. Now what, in your opinion,
    Must be our first step?

KATAI: Good question. We must, first of all,
    Sensitise and mobilise all those we intend to involve.
    That way, we will know their popular position
    As well as their individual positions regarding the issue.
    Then we can plan our strategy and work out
    The modalities how to execute it. It is like
    A coup d'état, you know.

SOKORO: It is not a coup d'état, da Katai.

KATAI: Don't you misconstrue me, da Sokoro.
    I'm not trying to attach anything negative to it.
    It is clearly a popular and just cause. Of course,
    Many are already fed up with the system:
    A system so despotic and so vicious and corrupt.
    Our only problem is who is ready and willing
    To take the bull by the horns. Think carefully.

SOKORO: I am ready. And I know and am convinced
    That you too are.

KATAI: Of course, I am.

SOKORO: Even Kenweng, on whom
    You cast your shadow of a doubt, is very prepared.

KATAI: How do you know this?

SOKORO: I don't think it would take me
    A battle to persuade him to join us.

KATAI: It is there, again, I fear. You tend to lean too
    Heavily on the wall of assumptions. What if your
    Method failed? What if he refused to see the need
    To support the cause? Remember, it is easy to walk
    A horse to a river, but...not as easy to force it to
    Drink of its water.

SOKORO: By implication, you mean that Kenweng will
    not
    Use his muscles even when he is faced with danger?

KATAI: You got me all wrong, da Sokoro.
    We want action and nothing but action. And not
    everyone
    Is so quick to action.

SOKORO: Listen, da Katai, don't you
    Underestimate Kenweng.
    Who has not heard the story of his muscles?
    Have you not seen him fight before?

KATAI [*Cynically.*]: We all call him Leopard.

SOKORO: Which, indeed, he is.

KATAI: True. But I witnessed a situation where
    He pulled out from — call it a clique to protest against
    An arbitrary levy imposed by the Chairman
    Of our so-called Clan Development Committee.

SOKORO: Ehn?

KATAI: The Chairman — I guess you know the story —
  He went round the clan himself. It was on a Sunday
  Evening, and his message was to announce
  To everyone that by Thursday that week
  Every man and woman would have paid
  To their respective quarter-heads
  What he described as CDL.

SOKORO: Yes. Clan Development Levy.
  Which could well stand for Common Debt Levy,
  For we all owe a debt of development.
  But CDL for what development project?

KATAI: Ask me what! He said emphatically
  That the levy must be paid on or before that Thursday,
  And that anyone who failed to comply
  Would be ostracised after being severely punished.

SOKORO: Ostracised?

KATAI: The very word he used. But no mention
  Was made of what project the clan was embarking on.

SOKORO: Same story.

KATAI: That's it. And each woman was to pay
  Half the levy of a man.
  I can't remember how much exactly,
  But everyone complained that the levy was high.

SOKORO: Wait a minute. Can you tell me what these men
   Have been doing with all the levies we've
   Been paying these many years?

KATAI [*Cynically.*]: Don't you see that
   The palace is beautiful?

SOKORO: What do you mean?
   So all these levies are meant to beautify the palace?

KATAI: How about the receptions organised
   For so and so officers who visited the clan?
   Or the so and so number of goats bought
   To meet and discuss so and so issues
   With so and so officers?

SOKORO: All lies! What has been the result
   Of all the huge expenditures?
[*Bluntly.*] They embezzle the money;
   Embezzlement is in their blood.
[*Indicating swearing.*] By the god of Thunder!

KATAI: But levies must be paid regularly,
   Or else you won't breathe the oxygen of the clan.

SOKORO: Glad I wasn't in
   When that particular levy was imposed.

KATAI: Lucky boy! Men sweated from head to toe.
   Especially those who had two, three, four wives,
   And had to pay for all of them or become a foe.
SOKORO: Na wa-o!

13

KATAI: But did this mean anything to the Chairman?
   You know, he is not married, has no children and,
   Perhaps, not even a girlfriend. *[Both laugh.]*
   So why should he have bothered?
   He has only one stomach to feed, and that is him.
[A pause.] Da, let me answer to the call of Nature.

[Exit KATAI.]

SOKORO *[Clicks his tongue.]*: What a fellow!
   I don't think there is any one on earth
   Who compares with Katai when it comes to
   Long discussions. I should have advised him
   To become a pastor. *[A pause. Thoughtfully.]*
   I must really talk to Kenweng. I think he is the only
     one
   Whom we can count on for proper action.
   We can't afford any further delay;
   This problem is long overdue.

[Enter KATAI.]

KATAI: But, as I said before, it would be wise to mobilise
   And sensitise the men we've identified, first of all.
   That way, we will be able to know
   Those who are really committed to the cause.
   While carrying out the mobilisation and sensitisation,
   We can then put up our demand for the Council to
     hold.
   This will lead on to our request for the General
     Meeting
   Everyone has been yearning for these many, long years.

In fact, this is how, in my humble opinion,
We should go about it. *[With emphasis.]* Step by step.

SOKORO: Perfectly correct, da Katai.
In fact, you have the wisdom of a man
Who has walked the long corridors of life.
I'm really lucky to have you as a friend.
Can you believe it? Since Obon Obini came to power,
He has always avoided general meetings.

KATAI: He does not want to show to the public
How clean his hands are.

SOKORO: Absolutely. His hands are too clean
For this clan. *[Getting emotional.]* But, da Katai,
We need an opportunity to genuinely and bluntly
Express our grievances against the system.
It is said that if you hide from an evildoer the evil he
does,
You have done the greater evil. We should make it
clear
To the King and his Council that we do not like the
Structure, that we are sick and tired of having kings
And councillors from virtually the same quarter
Of the clan generation after generation. Was the
Flag of Dynasty not burnt and the ashes thrown in
The confluence of Okpa-okomo roughly six Efeng
Festivals ago? And that is *[Calculating.]* seven times six,
Which is equal to forty-two years now. Incredible!
And nothing has changed; still the same structure,
The same system. And when you mention Dynasty,
They will tell you: No, no, no! Dynasty
Has been destroyed in the whole tribe.

No one should talk about it again.
It is now a thing of the distant past.

KATAI: This is sad! Trace the history and you will realise
That no king has ever ruled who is from
Our own quarter of the clan.
A meticulous look at the fine details will
Reveal that virtually the same family seems to have
been
Ruling this clan for over sixty years now.
It would appear no other family is good enough or
Capable enough to rule. And what is even more
Disturbing is the fact that the whole Council is
Nearly filled by the king's family.

SOKORO *[In a powerful outpour of emotions.]*:
And those who are prepared to eat the king's shit.
But this must change. Obini must be the last king
From that family, and he shall not wear his crown
To his dying days. We must crush the system;
We must trample on it; we must pound it into dust.

KATAI: Hold your breath, da Sokoro. It is not yelling
that...

SOKORO: You, da Katai—you have a way always
Of dampening my spirit with your foul tongue.
Do you consider me an empty braggart?
A megalomaniac? You know only too well that
My words are my bones; indeed, the driving-force
To my intended act.

KATAI *[In a praising tone.]:* Sokoro.

SOKORO: Bukai. Who can stand the taste of acid?
   I am Sokoro, the acidic one.

KATAI: Sokoro.

SOKORO: Bukai. I am he whose words have
   Corrosive powers, and drum on offending roofs
   Without ceasing. It is only God,
   The one whose chest is white and whose hands are
   Pure and clean, it is only He I fear.

KATAI: True. Your words have corrosive powers;
   You have a razor for tongue;
   Your frown sends down torrents of rain
   Even in the heart of the dry season.
   Power has been bestowed on you, da Sokoro.
[Emphatically.] By our ancestors. *[Both laugh.]*
   You have my respect and support, da Sokoro.

SOKORO: Da Katai, you are the fountain of my courage,
   The talisman of my indomitable power
   And the foundation on which
   The walls of my being are built.
   You are to me what the nest is to a wasp.
   The wasp returns to the nest for more power.

KATAI: I feel flattered, da Sokoro.

*[SOKORO swerves round abruptly. The two engage in a dumb
   display, communicating in the signs of a traditional society. Then
   they dance, first in one direction, and then in opposite directions,
   and finally facing each other. They feel so elated, and engage in*

17

a vigorous handshake, making each other stagger. They disengage after snapping their fingers. Then they slump into the old armchairs, laughing stupidly.]

KATAI: You are a man, indeed.

SOKORO: You, too, are a strong man. I didn't know
You could also communicate effectively in this language.

KATAI: Can you hold your head up in this clan
If you're dumb to the language of Ekwe?

[Enter OROKA. The FIGURE tiptoes out.]

OROKA: Breakfast is ready.

KATAI *[Looks up at the sun.]:* You call it breakfast? Look...

SOKORO: Leave the woman alone. *[To OROKA.]*
Did you sleep well, our wife?

OROKA: Yes. How about you?

SOKORO: All right. Except that your mbanya is not feeling
That well today.

OROKA: Oh! What's the problem?

SOKORO: Well...Not too bad though. Just a fever.
She'll soon be all right.

OROKA: Glad to hear that. I'll find time and see her.
SOKORO: Please, do. That'll be helpful.

OROKA *[To KATAI.]:* Should I bring it outside?

KATAI: No. We'll be right in.
[Exit OROKA.]

SOKORO: You should know how to respond to a woman
    In the morning, especially if you did not treat her well
    The previous night.

*[Enter MORUWA. He is clad in a colourful wrapper tied round
    the waist, the body exposed. He also wears a raffia turban richly
    studded with feathers of various colours, and carries two wooden
    rattles in both hands, which he shakes continually as he dances
    regally "singing" praises.]*

MORUWA: A'Moruwa! A'Moruwa! A'Moruwa!
    Moruwa, the Songbird of Ekon is out again.
    I can hear voices murmuring: Why is he out?
    What is happening? Please, don't you rack your brain
    To puzzle it out. Come close and get the message.
    Open your ears and listen to the Songbird. He bears
    A message from the great Leopard.

SOKORO: What message, Praise-singer?

KATAI: Let him set down his burden, da Sokoro.

SOKORO: A burden to distort the necks of slaves?

MORUWA *[Shakes his rattles.]:* Rain clouds

19

Assemble on the hills.
The wind bears them down, not makes them.
Moruwa carries messages from men of great heights.
He is out again, this time with a message from
He who roars and no cock crows.

SOKORO *[Charging towards him.]* : Stop that shit!
I am the cock that crows. Will you then stop
Singing your foolery.

KATAI: Pipe down, da Sokoro.
Give him time to set down his load, I say.
He is only one among the lot programmed to serve
He who claims to possess the whiskers of the Leopard.
[Pause.] In the land of rodents the pussycat is a Leopard.

MORUWA *[Takes a few strides away.]:* Blasphemy!
May the gods not listen to it. It is true, really true that
When the Leopard roars or black clouds gather
On the mountaintops, something must come to pass.
There must be some parched earth that needs
drenching
In order not for the polluting dust to be raised
By some stubborn wind.

SOKORO: What do you mean, Riddle-bag?

MORUWA: Moruwa did not come out to debate
Nor did he come out to fight. He is out to deliver
A message sent by the King.
[Yelling.] The King wants every man to his palace.
Immediately. That is the message.

SOKORO}: Another public execution?
KATAI   }: A clan of autocrats!

SOKORO: What is the problem, Praise-singer?

MORUWA: Just that is the message.

SOKORO: What? You mean public execution?

[Exit MORUWA in haste.]

KATAI *[After a long pause.]:* A heavy curse hangs
    On this clan.

SOKORO: There is no curse. We are the cause of
    Everything. It is said that the witch eats he who
    Is weak of voice. The problem with this clan is
    That we are surrounded by too many yes-men,
    Sycophants, stooges. Cowards, indeed, they are.

KATAI: You're perfectly right, da Sokoro.
    But if you heard them shout at their wives
    You would think they could
    Spit fire from their mouths, or break rocks
    With the vigour of their voices.

SOKORO: Cowardly husbands fight with their wives,
    A way to prove that they are men.

KATAI: And most of them are beaten by their wives,
    Who but raise cries to disguise their victory.
    In order to escape a fine by the female cult.
[Enter KENWENG.]

SOKORO: In the nick of time he comes!
Welcome, welcome, welcome, our great Leopard.

KATAI: Welcome, da Kenweng.
We've been dying to see you.

KENWENG *[Surprised.]:* What's going on here?
I just cannot...Didn't you get the message from the King?

SOKORO: Message of oppression?

KENWENG: *[Puzzled.]* What?

KATAI: We can't put up with it any longer.

SOKORO: We need a new Sun
And a new Moon in a new Sky.

KATAI: Ours should be a generation
That brings about the desired change.

KENWENG: What do you mean? Stop kicking me about!

SOKORO: A revolution.

KENWENG: What? It's all in riddles you speak.

KATAI: Now listen, da Kenweng. It is time we did not
Shut our eyes and mouths
When things continue to go wrong every day.
The problem of leadership in this clan.

Is no news to you.

KENWENG [*Nodding rather unconsciously.*]:
That's right, that's right.

KATAI: Although we are so used to the problems
That they are fast becoming part of our lives,
We must stand up for change.

SOKORO: That a tumour has developed so long in your
thigh
It may no longer hurt doesn't make it a part of your
body.

KATAI: Da Sokoro and I have been discussing the subject
Since morning. Who does not see nepotism in this
clan?
Who does not see favouritism? Who has not been
bruised
By the callused hands of victimisation and molestation?
Must we continue to condone all this?
It is time for change. Change to secure
Equal and human rights. [*A pause.*]
If we allow things to continue the way they do,
Our children are going to experience the worst forms
Of what we are experiencing today.

KENWENG [*Becoming conscious.*]: That is perfectly true.

SOKORO: Good. And this we must forestall.
We must destroy the system completely.
Today they move about, blowing their horns to the sky,
Telling the whole tribe that Dynasty has been
murdered

23

And buried with strong charms
So she wouldn't have the power of reincarnation;
And that any family now has the right to rule this clan.
But who does not see the ugly face of Dynasty?
Dynasty with piercing eyes like those of a hooting owl.
They think we do not see their monopoly in
 leadership?
They deceive themselves by taking us for bats,
Thinking that we are blind to their tricks
To always turn things around.

KATAI: So, da Kenweng, we need your support.
We all must put our heads and hands together
And come out with a strategy for the campaign.
If we try the easy way to put things on the right track
And fail, then we will have no choice but to employ
The most rigorous methods. Violence will solve it all.

KENWENG: Violence?

SOKORO: Yes. Sometimes violence is a necessary
 weapon.
Many tribes that enjoy peace today fought one war
After another. Peace is the rare commodity that
Every land strives to secure. Most often restored after
A bloody war. *[Stares into space for a while.]*
But can peace thrive in a soil of gross inequality
And injustice? A soil whose very grains are the
 fomenters
Of human abuse and wickedness? We must fight
against
Exploitation; we must fight against molestation; we
must

Fight against marginalisation and oppression. *[....]*
You are a strong man, da Kenweng.
There is no man in this clan who does not tremble
At the sight of your muscles when they swell out.
It is time you put them into proper use.

KATAI: Do not feel worried, da Kenweng.
I can see your face wears a horrid mask.
We are not going to use violence right away.
It will be the very last resort. Our first step would be
To press to hold a general meeting with the King.
We are sick and tired of PDCs.

KENWENG *[In a whisper, to SOKORO.]*:
What is meant by PDCs?

SOKORO *[Loudly.]*: Private dialogues and consultations.

KATAI: Everyone has been looking forward
To an open dialogue with the King *[In a cynical manner.]*
And his Most Royal Council. *[A short pause.]*
Only that will provide a good occasion
For the King to know our popular position
Regarding this age-long problem.
Perhaps he does not even know the problems
Facing this clan; perhaps no one cares to give him
The facts as they are. *[...]* This will be a good
 opportunity
For him to make a proper assessment of the situation.
Then he will cease to swim under the false illusion that
Because the palace breathes the clan lives.
The clan and the palace are two different worlds.

[A long pause.]

KENWENG *[Gives a deep breath.]:* Thank you very much
    For the wonderful plan. This has been the worry
    Of a cross section of people in this clan.
    There has been no freedom at all in the clan...

KATAI: Except for a selected few.

KENWENG: Yes thanks. But no freedom for the
    minority.
    Only exploitation. There is molestation;
    There is marginalisation, and you name the rest.
    Do we have a clan other than this one? Are we
    Strangers here? People complain in their farms;
    They complain in their toilets; they complain
    Behind closed doors. But no one has got the courage
    To express openly what so clearly disturbs the peace
    And retards progress in this clan.
    Everyone pretends to live in peace.

SOKORO: And we cannot continue to pretend;
    We cannot pretend to be happy.
    We cannot pretend to enjoy peace. The time is ripe -
    Even too ripe - for us to present our case
    And state our demand. *[To KENWENG, firmly.]*
    We count on your utmost cooperation.

KATAI: Da Kenweng, I'm really glad to note that you,
    too,
    Appreciate that this problem does exist.
    Which is the first step to solving the problem.
    Now we need many more like you. I mean those who
    Also identify the problem and are prepared to join
    In the campaign. Meet and talk to them. Explain

Everything to them. Then give us a feedback.
If we can succeed to win, say,
Ten more, then we can safely and confidently launch
The first phase of our campaign.

KENWENG: We are sure to have a good following.

[*SOKORO and KATAI walk aside, whispering.*]

SOKORO: What do you think about him?

KATAI: He is one of us already.

SOKORO: I told you, but your stubborn ears
    Would not allow you to hear.

KATAI: Let's not get into that again, da Sokoro.

SOKORO: We are going to have a good following.

KATAI: I hope and I pray.

SOKORO: Don't be pessimistic.
    Didn't you hear him say
    That people complain behind closed doors?
    Which means they, too, identify the problem,
    And are already fed-up with it.

[*Commotion from a distance.*]

KENWENG: Shall we go to the palace now.
    There seems to be some interesting discussion
    Going on there.

SOKORO: What interesting discussion
    Do you expect in this clan?
    Would you consider discussions to levy fines
    Or pronounce death sentences interesting?
    That's all the clan meets to discuss:
    What sort of punitive action to take.
[Loud applause and ululation offstage.]
    Maybe this time one of the King's men
    Is being given a new and greater title.

KATAI: When shall we ever be conferred with titles?

SOKORO: Are we not rebels? Do we deserve
    Any less or any more?

[More commotion, this time much louder.]

KATAI: Heard that? the message of the drum?
    Something is definitely wrong.
    We better rush in and have our breakfast.

[SOKORO and KATAI rejoin KENWENG. More commotion offstage.]

SOKORO: I wonder who is receiving
    A death sentence this time.

[Enter two MESSENGERS.]

1ST MESSENGER: We are here, gentlemen,
    Sent by His Highness
    To invite you to His Royal Presence.

2ND MESSENGER: He who wears the crown
    Wants to speak to Sokoro and Katai.

KENWENG: How about me?

SOKORO: Why do you want to receive a bullet
    That is not meant for you? The king wants to speak
    To Sokoro and Katai.

KATAI *[To MESSENGERS.]:* What is the matter?

1ST MESSENGER: Did you not hear the message
    Moruwa sang round the clan this morning?

KATAI: He said nothing, except that the king wanted
    Every man in his palace.

1ST MESSENGER: Yes. Kenweng and *[Pointing to*

SOKORO and the KATAI.] you both, like every other man,
    Are supposed to be there.

KATAI: But there was no special invitation
    Of Sokoro and Katai.

1ST MESSENGER: What we've brought you
    Is that special invitation you so desire.

SOKORO: Something wrong? *[KATAI nudges him
to shut up.]*

KATAI: Go tell the King we shall be there in a moment.

We were about to have our breakfast when you broke
in.

2ND MESSENGER: His Highness shall not see us
Without you.

SOKORO [*Agitated.*]: Then you have come to arrest us?
You have come to fight?

MESSENGERS [*In unison.*]: No.

[*OROKA peeps out; KATAI signals her to get back in. She
slams the door immediately after she disappears from sight.*]

KATAI: If you have not come to arrest,
If you have not come to fight, then
May I suggest that you excuse us.
We need to fill our stomachs
Just as you have filled yours.

MESSENGERS: We will wait.

[*SOKORO, KATAI and KENWENG exit into the house.*]

2ND MESSENGER: The men are so suspicious.

1ST MESSENGER: This should not surprise you.
They know what they have done, and that
They can't get off scot-free.
They've gone around saying all sorts of blasphemous
Things about His Highness. The most recent
Is their conspiracy to topple the Dynasty
Of His Most Royal Highness.

Time they reaped what they have sown.

2ND MESSENGER: Grasshoppers
Flapping their wings proudly in front of a brooding
hen.
Lead asking to share a room with fire.
These men, they are crazy. They want to melt
In the fiery hands of His Majesty.

[Enter SOKORO.]

SOKORO *[Furiously.]*: What did you say?
Say it again, if you are such courageous chicks
That you do not get unnerved at the sight of a kite.
I am Sokoro, the rock that melteth not,
The iron rod that bendeth not.
Dare you have the guts to open your mouths again
And say one more piece of shit,
And I'll break your stupid heads for you.

1ST MESSENGER: Save your head from the wrath of
His Royal Highness.

SOKORO *[Charging about dangerously.]*:
You have the guts to speak?
You have the strength of mind
To stare the Leopard in the face?
Save your heads! Save your heads
From the wrath of Sokoro,
You fools of the highest category.
I know you've spent all your lives
Cleaning the boots of your master.

[Enter KATAI and KENWENG.]

KATAI: What is the matter?

SOKORO: These men are trying to face
    The Leopard in a fight.

KATAI [To MESSENGERS.]: What the hell is going on
    here?
    Are you sure you are ready to face the consequence?

KENWENG: Have they come to pronounce the message
    Of the nipping of yet another sapling in the bud?
    They look like true Nsibidi of the King.

1ST MESSENGER [To KENWENG.]: I must advise
    You keep yourself out of this.
     Do not get entangled in a web
    That is not meant for you. That's the best I can offer
    you.

2ND MESSENGER: You are not known
    To be one of the rebels.
    Steer clear of this and save your head.

KENWENG: We are sick and tired of threats.
    Go tell the King to include my name on his list
    As one of the rebels. Rebellion is what the clan needs
    At this juncture to make it co-habitable
    By the so-called royal men and the non-royal men,
    The rich and the poor, the majority
    And the minority. Go and tell him. I'm not afraid.

SOKORO [To KATAI and KENWENG.]:

Tell these bootlickers
To save their heads from my hands.
Hot-and-bitter blood
Runs through my veins.

KATAI [*To MESSENGERS.*]: It is a pity, it is a real pity that
Your eyes can no longer see the wrong
And evil deeds the king does.
[*Facing the audience.*] I sincerely think that these men
Have been reduced to mere hunting dogs.

SOKORO [*To KATAI.*]:Ask these royal slaves
To quit my sight before I spit vengeance on their
heads.

KATAI: What a pity that you see your brothers exploited
And molested everyday, and all you do is give
Applause to that stone-hearted devil whose hands
Are as cold as Death's.

SOKORO [*Unconsciously.*]: And must this
Notorious devil continue to bathe in praises?

1ST MESSENGER: Then it is you we must praise?

[*Ululation offstage.*]

KATAI: Yet another given a title?
The king's men do swim in titles.

SOKORO [*Furiously.*]: Do you hear me, da Katai?
Or have they sealed your ears with wax of corruption?

Ask these men to quit my sight, or else...
I'll bring them face-to-face with Death.

2ND MESSENGER: We have not come to fight,
    Neither have we come to quarrel with anyone.

1ST MESSENGER: Let the hounds haunt their shadows.
    Our mission here is to take them
    To His Highness' presence.
    Do we bear arms for them to take our mission
    As invitation to a fight?

SOKORO: Did I hear you say hounds? You call us
    hounds?
    So it is we who are the hounds? It is we
    Who are the King's hunting dogs?
[Walks aside, facing the audience.] These are the dogs
    That eat nothing but clean, dry bones
    While their master's stomach is stuffed
    With chunks of meat.

2ND MESSENGER: We have come
    To take you to the palace;
    That's all we are here for.

SOKORO: That's all? Good. Then take this back with
    you.
    Tell the king that we will not come.

KATAI: Tell him we shall be there if and only if
    He makes a solemn promise that he will listen to us
    And to everyone that we shall invite.

KENWENG: Ask him to include my name on his list
     As one of the rebels demanding for change.

SOKORO: Tell him Sokoro will not come. Because the
     king
     Is known to have nothing to offer his people
     But doses of pain and suffering. Except for his men
     Who change titles the way chameleons change colour.

KATAI: Tell him—and take this point very seriously—
     Tell him that we are tired of private dialogues
     And consultations, and want an open dialogue with
     him.

[MESSENGERS take a few paces away.]

1ST MESSENGER: These men must be crazy.

2ND MESSENGER: They are, indeed, dreaming.

KENWENG: Tell him that he whose hands are pure and
     clean
     Is not afraid to wash them in a public stream.

1ST MESSENGER: All that we shall take to the King.

2ND MESSENGER: Dogs are happier with bones
     Than chunks of meat. But these men
     Are such a strange breed of dogs
     That they want but the master's share.

[Exit the MESSENGERS.]

SOKORO [*Angrily.*]: What has that idiot just said?
KENWENG   : That dogs...[*Stops.*]
KATAI   :

KATAI: That dogs are happier
    With bones than chunks of meat. [*A short pause.*]
    So you can see what sort of men the king has.

KENWENG: Finished men. Stooges.
    Yes-men. Hand-clappers.

SOKORO [*Pacing back and forth.*]:
    We should have crushed them,
    Should have crushed them like watermelons.
    Instead of bandying words with the stooges,
    Instead of wasting our precious breaths
    With the less-than-beasts.
    Come on comrades! Let us plan a quick strategy.
    Look up at the hills yonder.
    Can you see the thick, dark clouds crawling down?
    Do you know what they portend?
    Witch clouds on their mission to conceal
    The evil deed the Devil King is about to do. [*A pause.*]
    I foresee something terrible. My blood speaks to me.
    It warns me in very stringent terms.
    We must be armed immediately.
    And should be prepared and ready to die if we must.
    Provided that the land is left safe and free
    From that tyrant's yoke. Our aim should be to take
    The crown off that devil's head, and make him
    Stare at Death with childish fright.
    We must be armed and ready to fight the fight.

KATAI: There shall be no fight.

SOKORO: Stop! Must we stand here armless
      Like brainless men? Why, if you throw a bomb
      You expect an explosion.

KENWENG: Ikpok-obi has her mouth open always.

SOKORO: To swallow who?
      I will transform into a porcupine and,
      With my quills, I will tear his greedy throat.
[In an imperious tone.] We must be armed, I say.

KATAI: Do not work yourself into frenzy, da Sokoro.

SOKORO: Do not be slow of thought, da Katai.
      What has transpired between the King's dogs and us
      Is enough to set the whole clan ablaze. Don't you
        know
      What our king is capable of? No chances!
      No taking things for granted!

KENWENG: I share the same view with you, da Sokoro.
      After a heavy downpour you cannot dispute
      That there will be a flood in the river.
      Are you a stranger here, da Katai?

KATAI: Nothing will happen. *[….]* Bet here?
      Do you think the Leopard never trembles?
      Why, even the Earth does tremble.
      He knows that we maintain a firm ground,
      And so must take his time.

SOKORO: You must be dreaming, da Katai.

KENWENG: We should not take things for granted.
It is better we were armed and nothing happened,
Than otherwise.

[Sound of ululation, seemingly approaching.]

SOKORO: Did you hear that?
The Leopard searching for a goat to tear.

KENWENG: Let's get ourselves organised
To face the impending battle.
The Sky seems to frown on the Earth.

[Exit KATAI.]

SOKORO: Da Katai sometimes is slow to act.
We do not have to take chances. Why, a man setting
out
On a long journey through a jungle must be armed
And fully prepared. We are on a difficult journey
To save this land.

KENWENG: Da Katai is best known
For his unending arguments.
He often makes light of very serious matters.
I must go and get myself ready.

SOKORO: You can't, I'm afraid, you can't.
It's too late now. We'll certainly get
All that we need from Katai.

[Enter KATAI, with three long cutlasses.]

KENWENG: Give me mine.

KATAI: Not until I've performed the necessary ritual.

SOKORO: What ritual? Unnecessary procrastination!

KATAI *[Holding up the cutlasses.]:* The gods of the land,
    The spirits of our departed heroes, it is on you we call.
    We know your eyelids never meet, and that day and
     night
    You keep a keen eye on what is going on in this clan.
    The time has come for us to ask
    For your abundant blessings.
    Give us undaunted courage so that we face
    What now seems to make our hearts beat so with
     fright.
    Send us your avenging hand to guide and lead us
    Through this trying moment.

SOKORO *[Interrupting.]:* Amen.

KENWENG: Amen.

KATAI: We are out for freedom fight.
    Freedom fight is fight for all, and fight for all
    Must be fought by all. Do not leave us to fight alone.
    Join us in your numbers. May you also encourage our
    Brothers to join us so that we can have every strength
    And might to subdue those power-drunk devils.

SOKORO: Exactly.

KENWENG: Obasi a' bukei—the land god—hear us.

SOKORO: But we do not have time to waste
   On long supplications. May the gods protect us.

KENWENG: Amen.
KATAI [*Ignoring.*]: Shower your blessings
   On your suffering children.
   Protect us from the devil's hand.

SOKORO [*Loudly.*]: Stop.

KENWENG: Yes.

SOKORO: A pastor who does not know the way
   To the shrine. Do you want to turn this moment
   Into a sermon?

KENWENG: The gods have heard our prayer.
   Long prayers only strain their ears.

[*A sudden blast of drums, so close that everyone trembles. Enter
   MORUWA. SOKORO and KENWENG immediately
   snatch a cutlass each from KATAI who now looks so
   confused.*]

KATAI: Is it time enough for us to act? I see but Moruwa,
   A mere Praise-singer. Where are the King's warriors?

MORUWA: A'Moruwa! A'Moruwa! A'Moruwa! [*He stops,
frightened at the sight of the cutlasses now held high.*]
   Moruwa is not out for war,
   Nor to pronounce a message of war.
   He is here to announce the outing of the Leopard,
   The one who roars and no cock crows.

40

SOKORO [*Confronting MORUWA.*]: Hold that shit!
   Keep it to yourself. And, I must warn,
   Be wise and save your head by dancing
   Your foolery back to your master, the one
   Whose shit is your food.
[*To KATAI.*] Shit has taken the place of this man's brain.

KATAI: True, like the lobster, he carries shit in his head.

KENWENG: What an attribute! [*Sneeringly.*]
   The one who roars and no cock crows.
   Is it because ours is not a clan of crowing cocks?
[*To MORUWA, furiously.*] Must a python roar
   Before you are convinced that it can kill?
   Don't you let the python swallow you.

[*MORUWA is perplexed and terrified. He turns back
   immediately, visibly trembling, but without shaking his rattles
   nor uttering a word. Enter two elderly men, each carrying a long
   spear on his shoulder. They are OSERE and AKPARIKA.
   SOKORO, KATAI and KENWENG charge at them
   immediately they make an entrance, but this does not unnerve
   them one bit.*]

OSERE [*In an imperious tone.*]: Stop! I command you
   To stop and stand still! Stop! I say. We have not come
   For war. [*SOKORO, KATAI and KENWENG bring
   down their cutlasses.*] What is the matter with you?
   Have you lost your minds? Your veins do seem
   To bathe in hot blood. I can see you are poised and
   ready
   For some terrible act, too terrible for this land.
   May the gods bring you back your minds.

May this land enjoy peace. *[A pause.]*
I must warn you, my sons, think again.
Think like the book men that you are.
Do not allow yourselves to be ruled by strange
  ambitions.
You may falter and fall into a pit where you will lie
Buried and forgotten forever. And you will not enjoy
The new dawn and the new sunshine which are yet to
  see
This side of our mountain. *[In a mumbling tone.]*
When I see our young men showing
Such uncommon courage, I feel like shedding tears,
I feel like weeping like a child.

AKPARIKA: What are you talking about, da Osere?

OSERE *[Ignoring the question. To the young men.]*:
  No war! No bloodshed! For you know not
  What lies buried right where you stand.
  The tree has seen seasons come and go. No war!
*[OSERE and AKPARIKA bring the tips of their spears together
  and lower them gradually to the ground, forming a V-shape as
  they hold the wooden ends. KATAI, SOKORO and
  KENWENG look on with awe.]*

AKPARIKA *[To the young men, in a cruel tone.]*:
  You can't go to war with the clan, can you?
  Which means you can't go to war with the King.
  Because the King is the clan.
  He is the voice of the gods; he is the voice of our
  Ancestors; he is the voice of the clan.

SOKORO *[Almost barking.]*: He is not the voice of the

clan.

OSERE: Hold your peace.

[OSERE and AKPARIKA hold their spears pressed against their left flanks, the pointed ends pointing to the sky.]
SOKORO: He is the voice of exploitation.

OSERE: Stop! I say.

SOKORO: He is the voice of molestation and torment.

OSERE *[As SOKORO continues ranting, shaking his head.]*:
    There is something terribly wrong with this man, I
    guess.

SOKORO: He is the voice of marginalisation.
    He is not and cannot be the voice of the clan.

KATAI *[Sarcastically.]*: He is the voice of his bunch
    Of yes-men, of course.

SOKORO: Thank you, da Katai,
    For the wonderful correction.
    The king has succeeded to fence himself with a bunch
    Of yes-men. They are his bodyguards...and slaves.

OSERE: Listen, my sons. Listen to me.
    Hearken to my advice.
    Think like book men. Think before you act
    And do not act before you think. You may act
    wrongly.
[Brief silence.] The King is on his way to speak to you.

He may not sound polite,
But listen to him and be humble.

KATAI: Thank you, Koko Osere, for the advice. It is you
We respect. But permit us to state in very clear terms
That we are out for no compromise that brings no
change.
The system must change.
The wind of change blows!
Although in eddies of cowardice.

KENWENG: No. There are strong currents of
determination
Cutting through, paving a way for the desired change.

SOKORO: Change in the interest of all,
Not in favour of a few, mind you.

AKPARIKA: Why all this talk about change?
What is wrong with the system?

SOKORO: You will never find anything wrong.
Your eyes are trained not to see any fault.

KATAI: It is a pity that things go wrong
Unnoticed even by men of your own age and wits.
A clear sign of a great misfortune;
It portends a devastating flood.

[Silence.]

SOKORO: Koko Osere, I can see you listen with a keen
ear.

We are not mad; there is nothing wrong with our
heads.
The simple fact is that we want change.
The present system is so cruel and so partial,
Do you need to be told this?

OSERE [*Takes a deep breath.*]: Well, my sons.
We have heard all that you have said.
But, as they say, if your eyes are too open,
You see the devil; if your ears are too open,
You hear curses, and if your mouth is too open,
You swallow a wasp. It is sometimes advisable
To be foolish, or to feign foolishness.
Because by being or appearing to be foolish,
You are sure to get what you need. [*…*] If you look
round,
You will see what I am talking about.
Many men have risen to positions of power
Because they appeared to be foolish
Before their masters. They say if you know how to rub
The back of a tortoise, it will dance for you.
No two leopards can occupy the same territory.

SOKORO: Thank you very much, Koko Osere.

KATAI: Thank you, Koko, for your kind advice.

KENWENG: Thank you, wise one, for the brilliant
sayings.

SOKORO: Who does not know that old age
Comes with wisdom? [*To OSERE.*] But...[*Grins.*] do
You beg for what belongs to you? [*Emphatically.*]

It is our right, our legitimate right, to demand for
  change.
Why do we have yesterday and today and tomorrow,
And not yesterday alone?
Because there must always be a new day.
It is so obvious that we of this clan
Wear the shoes of yesterday to dance to the music
Of today. It can't work, I'm afraid, it simply can't.

AKPARIKA [*Cynically.*]: And this thing you call change,
  Does it come like a rush of wind?

KATAI [*Firmly.*]: No single individual must decide
  The destiny of all. We now stand up for radical change.

KENWENG: Yes. Every living society desires change.

[*A pause.*]

SOKORO: Koko Osere, once again, thank you.
  Thank you, too, Koko Akparika.
  You both have our respect.
  You are amongst the most intelligent elders we have.
  That is why we respect you. But.
  I will like you to mark this.
  We, I mean, especially, da Katai and I,
  Do not see and appreciate things
  In the same way as you do. [*Laughing mockingly.*]
  We did not spend all these many years in school
  For nothing. We did, at least, acquire something new.
  Something that you the old men will never acquire
  In your lifetime. [....] Our eyes are now open.
  And we now can see what you definitely cannot.

46

OSERE [*Nodding,, in near cynicism.*]: That is very true.
   My son used to sit down, looking at a paper
   And talking to himself like a fool.

SOKORO [*In a retort.*]: He is no fool.
   He communicates with papers
   Just the way you commune with the gods and
      ancestors.
   But your ways are old and wily ways.
   We can look at a paper
   And tell you precisely what is happening in distant
      lands.
   A paper, by looking at it,
   Can teach us how to do great things.

AKPARIKA [*Unconsciously.*]: Whiteman's witchcraft!

KATAI: Yes. Not the evil type you practise here.

SOKORO: That is why we need change.
   Many clans have changed their old ways, and
   You need to see what is going on there.
   Some already have good roads,
   And people now make their journeys riding long cars
   Instead of trekking and sweating
   And kicking toes against tree roots
   And tumbling over stones. [*A pause.*]
   It takes them less than an hour
   To do the same distance as from here to Anaku.

KATAI: We need progress. We need development.
   And there is no development without change.
   Of course, development itself is change!

47

SOKORO: Radical change!

KENWENG: Change for the good of all.

OSERE: Now listen...

SOKORO: Change is all we need, dear elders.

KATAI: Change, change, and nothing but change!

[Brief silence.]

KENWENG: Let's listen to what the wise one has to say.

SOKORO: Provided it is something
    That favours our cause.

[A pause.]

OSERE: A wise man uses his head,
    Not his fists.

[A sudden blast of drums. Exit OSERE and AKPARIKA.]

SOKORO: The moment to test our courage draws near.

[Exit KATAI, taking his cutlass with him.]

KENWENG: Why did he leave?

SOKORO: To get things set, I guess.

KENWENG: But we are already armed.

SOKORO: Perhaps to wear his charms.

KENWENG: Hmm. I think...

SOKORO: What?

KENWENG: I sincerely think the men did tell us a lot.

SOKORO: A lot of nonsense and little sense.

KENWENG: Osere is a clever man.

SOKORO: By your own standard.

[Enter KATAI with an old spear.]
KATAI: Nothing wheels us from our course;
   We must stand our ground and fight the cause.

SOKORO: We maintain our stand with all firmness.

*[KATAI holds up the spear. KENWENG AND SOKORO
gaze at him in amazement.]*

KATAI *[Addressing the spear.]*: May you
   Obey my command. To the last word, to the last letter.
[A pause.] My grandfather gave you to me when I was
   born.
   You were kept under my bed until I learnt to walk.
   Perhaps that I may grow into a warrior,
   A militant, a freedom-fighter.
[He kisses the spear.] Time you proved your potency.

KENWENG: But, gentlemen, I think we must think

again.
What Koko Osere said is pregnant with meaning.
We may not have to be so radical in our approach.
They say he who bends in a wind survives a storm.

KATAI: Now you speak like a coward.
[To SOKORO.] I did express my doubts
When you told me about him.
I do not doubt his physical strength but, I'm afraid,
He is such a man that he trembles
In the slightest breath of wind.
I know him; that is why I fear that
We may meet with some disappointment.

SOKORO [To KENWENG.]: Don't you disappoint me.
I have built a lot of confidence in you.
You have proven, on several occasions,
That you are a man. But to be a man
Is not merely by the use of muscles to subdue. It is by
The strength of will. A man stands by his words,
No matter what.

[A short pause.]

KENWENG [Walks aside, facing the audience.]: If you see
A tree swaying so flexibly in the wind,
Your conclusion may be that it is soft of wood.
But...it is the axe that tells the wood,
Not the eyes. Why, Nature has a way
Of puzzling the mind. Look at your palms.
Look at them again and yet again. Do it, everyone, do
it.
Of course, you do this every blessed day,

From the day you were born.
Now imagine that a thief rushed at you and cut off
Those hands of yours, and was later arrested.
You are asked to appear in court
To identify and collect your hands
From amongst seven pairs.
Can you tell which pair are yours?

[A sudden blast of drums, followed by ululation. Enter OBON OBINI, preceded by OSERE and AKPARIKA. Six GUARDS follow OBON OBINI very closely. A host of other men, including the DRUMMERS, bring up the rear. MORUWA snakes his way in and out of the crowd as he performs his usual ritual dance. SOKORO, KATAI and KENWENG take a defensive stance.]

OSERE *[In a loud voice.]:* The gods forbid that! His Royal Highness is here to speak to you. All you must do is listen.

[SOKORO and KENWENG place their cutlasses on the ground beside them; KATAI pins his spear on the ground in front of him. MORUWA walks up defiantly and stands facing them.]

MORUWA *[Shakes his rattles.]:*
He who roars and no cock crows
Is around. *[Rattles.]* He whose claws can tear
The hide of an elephant has come. *[Rattles.]* He
Whose voice, like thunder, can break the hardest rock
Is here. *[Rattles.]* He who is second to none
In the whole clan. *[Rattles.]* The one who bathes in a basin
Held high by strong arms, His Royal Highness Obon

51

Obini
Of the line of Leopards has walked his way
To your humble presence.
The cock has crowed. The Sun has torn
The thick blanket of Night: it is dawn.

[He dances regally to the left, to the right, back and forth
and then stands facing OBON OBINI who is now flanked
by OSERE and AKPARIKA, both holding up their spears.
All the rest fall behind .OBON OBINI acknowledges the
performance by raising his royal staff and shaking it
slightly. A blast of drums.]

Your Royal Highness
The Pride of Korup,
The great Leopard reared and groomed
In the ancient settlement of Kitok *[Drums.]*,
Kitok that towers on the highest peak of Nwaak,
The womb of the great tribe of Korup,
The home of our ancestral spirits and land gods,
The mother of the line of Leopards,
The symbol of power and dignity. *[Drums.]*
Obon Obini of the Royal family,
He who coughs out thunder and spits out fire,
[Ululation.] He who roars and no cock crows.
Obini Obini the great,
Here you face the gentlemen
Who claim to stare without blinking.

[Drums and ululation. MORUWA takes his place beside
OSERE. Terrifying silence. OSERE looks up, down and then
about him as though searching for an invisible being. Then...]

OSERE: I fear for this clan. *[Grumbling from the crowd.]*
I have lost nearly every dream I had for this clan.
What I have left are but frightful nightmares. *[A mix of grumbling and motion of support.]*

AKPARIKA: Don't you let the gods hear
Those awful utterances.

OSERE *[Ignoring the comment.]*: I say times have changed.
What we see today was never seen before;
What we hear today was unheard of;
What we do today was, in the good old days,
Considered taboo. *[A pause.]* There is a fast decay
Of our cultural bedrock.
Our traditions are almost a heap of ruins.
[Emotionally.] Who could violate the bidding of His Royal
Highness? Who could look at the King in the face
When he speaks? Was there anyone?
[In a mumbling tone.] Could it be ignorance
Or impudence that has pushed us
To cause things to change so?
Have we lost our minds?
[In a vigorous tone.] Do we know
We are challenging the gods?
Do we know we are spitting insults on our ancestors?
Do we know we are inviting
The most catastrophic whirlwind of Efeng
To invade this already tilting clan?
Doom is near; the angels of doom hover around.
The sky has turned red: the blue is gone.
All the messengers of benevolent gods have
disappeared.
The air is stuffy and choking. *[To OBON OBINI.]*

Your Royal Highness, excuse my impudence
To have kept you waiting as I spoke.
Your heart be filled with mercy!
These young men who are standing in front of you
Like frightened lizards are certainly dreaming.
They must have eaten some strange herb
That has upset their feeble brains.
They are mad. Tolerance, your Royal Highness,
 tolerance!
Have mercy on the ignorant young men.

AKPARIKA [*Angrily.*]: Stop!
They have committed the most grievous offense,
And you open your mouth to suggest His Royal
Highness should show mercy? If truly they were mad
They would sleep in gutters and on refuse heaps.
But these mad, young men, they still share the same
 beds
With their wives. [*A pause.*] Now they speak blasphemy
Against His Royal Highness.
Must we then, since you say they are mad,
Let them go scot-free? [*...*] If I were the King
I would command my soldiers
To have them all hanged.
Or for Nsibidi to take their heads.

SOKORO: For speaking blasphemy against the King?
 And what blasphemy? What is it you call blasphemy?

AKPARIKA: They call themselves *book* men. Is it that
 Book makes men drunk with rudeness?

SOKORO [*Emotionally.*]: You must keep the rest

Back in your stomach. If all elders were like you
We would have been forced
To turn this land into a boiling sea of Okpa-okomo.
You are one of the perpetrators of evil in this clan.

KATAI [*Tapping SOKORO on the back.*]: Hold your peace.

SOKORO: I hold no peace. All the devils in this clan,
  Doom awaits them. May it be meted out to them
  What they mete out to others! Blood for blood;
  Cruel death for cruel death.

[*A blast of drums; this stops abruptly. MORUWA steps out and
  shakes his rattles in order to restore quiet. Silence.*]

MORUWA: This clan has ever been a dignified clan.
  From the very day it came out of the womb of Kitok.
  This is where all the rivers that wash the entire land
  Of Korup meet. In the mighty sea of Okpa-okomo,
  The great city of the supernatural,
  The treasure of the riches of every earthly tribe.
  It is here important discussions of the tribe are held.
  Judgement on criminals who have
  Committed serious crimes
  Cannot be passed in any other clan in the tribe.
  This is the home of Ikpok-obi,
  The bottomless depression that has swallowed
  Thousands on thousands of...

AKPARIKA: Stop! [*Clears his throat meaningfully. In near
whisper.*] A man bridles his tongue when he speaks.
[*Loudly.*] His Royal Highness has cleared his throat.
  No one speaks.

[Ululation. MORUWA walks back to where he stood; that is beside OSERE. Perfect silence.]

OBON OBINI: When I look up at the sky,
    At the changing clouds,
    I see nothing, nothing but strange stars.
    Stars that cast shadows across the entire sky.
    So our land may see less light and more darkness?
    Yet I hear this stupid talk about change;
    Change in darkness?
[To the young men.] If change be what you desire,
    young men,
    Why then do you cast shadows
    Across the sky of things?
    Why do you go on insulting our ancestors
    And the gods of fortune?
    You are the stars
    That bring darkness to this clan.

[A mix of grumbling and motion of support; and then a clear voice offstage.]

VOICE *[Loudly and tremulously.]:* All stars dispel darkness.

AKPARIKA: Stop! The Leopard roars.

OBON OBINI: You are right, whoever spoke.
    But there are stars also of darkness,
    And these are the stars I speak about.
    Stars that stand in the way of our sacred traditions.
    They will be burnt by the Giant Star.
    And their ashes we shall take
    To the great sea of Okpa-okomo.

[A long pause.] When I place my ear on the ground
 And listen to the sound from the forest, I wish I were
  dead
 Before this day. For what I hear, no ear on the
 Royal Stool, in the whole line of Leopards in this land,
 Has ever heard before. Terrible sound, too terrible,
 Especially for one who has not held a brush nor
  touched
 A piece of soap with his fingers since his birth.
[A terrifying sound is heard. Everyone but OBON OBINI
trembles with great fear.] What a strange sound!
 Like a million rivers racing across each other.
 Or like some mad brooks rushing uphill.
 But who will win the race? What a mad race!
 What a mad crop of crazy creatures!

KENWENG *[Unconsciously.]*: We will win.

OBON OBINI *[Surveys around, ferociously.]*: Who spoke?

MORUWA: Your Highness, Kenweng,
 The one who wants his name added
 To the list of rebels,
 It was he who spoke.

OBON OBINI: What effrontery! Foolhardiness!
 Akparika, take him behind at once
 And show him the Leopard's claws.

[AKPARIKA and four GUARDS seize hold of KENWENG.
 There is a serious scuffle as the five struggle to take
 KENWENG away.]

OBON OBINI: Take him away! You are weaker
    Than cocoyam stems. *[Loudly.]* Hurry up!
    You...the two of you, bring his hands behind him
    And hold them firm. Then you there...
    See how they stagger like drunken bulls!
    Ofofo has burnt every tissue of their muscles.
    Thunder strikes me dead! How, for goodness' sake,
    Can a single man torment five men? *[He dashes forward*
and makes to strike KENWENG with his staff but stops.]
    The gods forbid! I want him tortured and left alive
    To suffer the pain. *[A short pause.]*
    You there...fall behind him. And push. Push him away.
    Pu-u-ush! That's right. Go on, push! Take the idiot
    away!

[SOKORO, who is already writhing with anger, charges at OBON
    OBINI as KENWENG is being carted away. OBON
    OBINI steps aside in self-defence and stands staring at
    SOKORO with the ferocity of a leopard.]

1ST VOICE: Has insanity gripped the mind of this clan?

2ND VOICE: This has never happened before. It must be
    The dawn of a new era, the beginning of...

SOKORO: This cannot happen before my eyes,
    Not when I still maintain my sight. The devil must see
    Yet another devil. *[Facing OBON OBINI.]*
    Devil king, wicked king!
    You whose hands are colder than Death's.
    You still bear the burning spear
    Of that most cruel ambition?
    Your reign has brought untold sufferings to this clan.

Many a young man has received torments
From your cruel hands. Many more have disappeared,
Leaving behind no graves, no sign
Of their erstwhile existence in this ailing land. This clan
Will see no progress and will enjoy no peace
And no freedom while you mount the Royal Stool.

[*SOKORO gets so emotional that he is caught between tears and speech.*]

OBON OBINI: Speak! Tell me more.

[*SOKORO rushes back and picks up his cutlass. At once two GUARDS grip him from behind. Ululation amid lashing sound offstage. KATAI paces back and forth, apparently confused. He picks up his cutlass and throws it down again. He pulls out the spear from the ground and throws it at a wall. He is so restless. SOKORO now faces OBON OBINI for trial. Lashing sound continues.*]

1ST VOICE: The Leopard
    Must be devouring the goat very badly.

OBON OBINI: Thank you, my good men.
    A goat wants to fight
    With the Leopard. Osere, take him at once to my
    palace
    And teach him how to be rude to the King.

[*SOKORO is dragged away amid lashing sound.*]

1ST VOICE: What a clan!

2ND VOICE *[In near whisper.]*: What will happen to him?

[KATAI walks up to the King.]

KATAI: Your Royal Highness the King of Ekon,
    Our land is sinking deep into the mire.
    Of the most cruel crime. The depth increases
    Each time you raise your torturing hand.
    The land will soon collapse and get buried, and...
    We shall all perish. Those who died by the torment
    Of your hand shall rise again.

OBON OBINI *[Puzzled.]*: Shall rise again?
KATAI: Yes, shall rise again...and fight
    Till these old, cruel ways
    Are destroyed; till every voice in this land
    Shall sing but freedom song,
    And every single soul shall cease to slave.
[A short pause.] You swim in a pool of deceit,
    Your Highness. No one tells you the truth.
    All these men standing here,
    Who, when on you they shower their false praises
    And make you feel like one raised to the Heavens
     above,
    To meet and dine with Angels and Saints,
    They deceive you. You stick so deep
    In the most cruel sin that the Gates
    Of Heaven are closed on you.

OBON OBINI *[Casts KATAI a venomous look.]*:
    Are you sure, young man,
    That there is nothing wrong with your head?
    You are inviting the most bitter

Of all the pronouncements - slow death!
Don't you make me give instructions to that effect.

KATAI: All those men giving you their false support,
They grumble in their stomachs;
They, too, demand for change.
No one is happy with what is going on here.

1ST VOICE: No one!

OBON OBINI [Furiously.]: Who spoke? Let him who
spoke
Step forward and show me his bold face.
[Silence, but for the lashing sound.] If you want to join
This crop of rebels, do it now. I say, now!
[He holds MORUWA by the arm and walks aside, talking
angrily to himself.] This clan needs proper raking.
I will rake them all out! To the last grain. [He stops.]
It seems I'm surrounded
By the most treacherous snakes.
[To MORUWA.] Did you see who spoke?

MORUWA: Your Highness, I saw no one.
Only heard a voice from among the group.

OBON OBINI [Thunderously.]: Voice of a coward!
[Walking back.] Akparika! Akparika!

AKPARIKA [Offstage.]: Carrying out your order,
Your Highness.

OBON OBINI: Bring the goat back here.

AKPARIKA: Yes, Your Highness.

OBON OBINI: Goats challenging the Leopard to a fight.
[In a cruel, grating tone.] I will tear them all up
   And show them how many flimsy muscles
   Constitute their deceitful bulks.

[Enter KENWENG, with hands tied behind him. His shirt is torn and smeared with blood. AKPARIKA and the four GUARDS follow closely behind . KATAI becomes more restless.]

KATAI: The great King of Ekon,
   I await my turn.
OBON OBINI: The wages of rudeness is punishment.
   Corporal punishment, not banishment.
   He who challenges the Leopard
   Is devoured by the Leopard.
[To AKPARIKA.] Go and push him down.
   Let him lie down flat on the ground like a lizard.
   Let the dolt show me how bold and strong he is.

[KENWENG is laid flat on the ground.]

OBON OBINI: Pour water on him. Someone,
   Go fetch some water. Immediately.

[Exit MORUWA. Immediately OSERE and the two GUARDS enter.]

KATAI: What a cruel land!
   When shall we be free from all these torments?

OBON OBINI: Shut your mouth! *[To OSERE, in a whisper.]* Taken care of?

OSERE: Yes, Your Highness. And, I must report,
    The young man stood fearless and trembled not
    At the sight of the instrument that was to take off
    His crown. He only smiled and said: May my blood
    Wash away the swamps.

OBON OBINI: Stupid talk! Talk of a coward!
    Show me the sign that the deed is done,
    You cocoyam stem.

OSERE *[Showing his bloodstained palms.]*: Here,
    Your Highness,
    Pure and stainless blood of youth.

OBON OBINI *[Angrily.]*: Blood of rudeness!
    He who is rude to the Leopard
    Shall be devoured by the Leopard.
    I shall tolerate no rudeness from anyone.
    No one shall question the Leopard. No one!

KATAI: May my turn come, Your Highness.

OBON OBINI: Your turn comes. *[Erie silence.]*
    Your rudeness has been beyond compare.
    I feel like jumping at you and tearing you up.

KATAI: Yes, your Highness. I'm ready.

OSERE *[Casting KATAI a cautionary look.]*: Stop!
    The Leopard roars.

[A pause.]

OBON OBINI: Clearly, you were dragged into the pit.
  And now you stand there pouring lumps of earth
  Over your head to bury you up? Foolhardiness!
  What a foolish cock you are that you flaunt your red
   crest
  In front of a fox! *[….]* I pity you so much. *[Aside.]*
   When I
  Look at the tributaries that flow into the stream
  That nurtured me into being, I see him
  As a visible strand in the network. *[Loudly, rather
  unconsciously.]*
  Thus I pity him...with all my heart.
  The King, too, has a heart of pity.
  He who deserves mercy receives mercy. *[A short pause.
  To KATAI.]* An inner voice keeps telling me...
  Oh how it weakens the muscles of my tongue
  To soften it all for you. *[A pause.]* You have
  The rare privilege to enjoy the leniency of justice
  In this clan.

1ST VOICE: Clever act! No King is known
  To point his wrathful sword
  At one who is near by blood.

[Grumbling from the CROWD, then silence.]

OBON OBINI: Who spoke?

OSERE: Coward, my Lord, same coward.

[Enter MORUWA, carrying a small basin. He pours the water

over KENWENG. OBON OBINI looks on. Ululation.]

OSERE: The wages of rudeness to a king.

OBON OBINI *[As MORUWA is walking back.]*: Good
   soldier.
   Thank you. *[....]* Thank you. *[A short pause.]*
   Now back to you, young man.
   You will give us, here and now, two bottles of *ofofo*.
[A throb of drums.] Then tomorrow, you shall cook
   For the Royal Council two limbs of bush pig
   And a basin of plantains. Four bottles of *ofofo*
   Shall be used to wash down the food.
   Now the two bottles. Quick! *[Yelling.]* Ojei babab
   Korup!

ALL: Owa!

*[Exit KATAI. Traditional music and dancing. MORUWA goes
   on with his ritual display, yelling: "A'Moruwa", etc. OBON
   OBINI dances regally on the same spot. Then after a few
   moments, he "kills" the display by dashing out smartly and
   pounding his staff on the ground in front of the group of
   DRUMMERS. Drumming stops abruptly.]*

OBON OBINI *[Striking his chest.]*: I remain the King
   Of this clan. Let those who have large mouths
   And long tongues go on talking; let them speak
   Against the Royal Throne. And Nsibidi, the spirits of
   war,
   Shall unhinge their jaws one by one. Their tongues
   Shall be pulled out and thrown to the fowls of the air.

[Enter KATAI.]

AKPARIKA: Ojei, ojei, ojei babab Korup!

ALL: Owa!

AKPARIKA: Ojei, ojei, ojei babab Ekwe!

ALL: Owa!

AKPARIKA: Oho-ho-o-o!

ALL: Oho-o-o-o-o!

[Ululation. AKPARIKA walks up to and collects the two bottles from KATAI. He walks back, smiling, and stands in front of OBON OBINI.]

AKPARIKA: Here, your Highness, are the two bottles
From the young man. The rest of the fine shall be paid
Tomorrow. *[To KATAI.]* You hear? Before the sun
Goes to bed. *[He presents the bottles to OBON OBINI*
who touches them with his fingers. Then he bellows.]
Ojei, ojei babab bario!

ALL: Owa!

[A pause.]

OBON OBINI: We have left out two important items.
The Leopard must crunch a kola with his teeth
And tear a cock with his claws. *[Drums.]* This done
To appease the gods and spirits of our ancestors.

[To KATAI.] Take note. Four kola nuts and a cock
    To be included. Bring the cock alive. Of course,
    You know the tradition, don't you?
    Our traditions must be maintained;
    Our culture must be kept intact.
    Whoever attempts to bring ruin
    On what has so clearly stood the test of time
     generation after generation,
    Simply invites ruin on himself. Shall go where others
    Of his crop and kind have gone.
[Drums.] Our land must enjoy peace, perfect peace.
    Our traditions must remain holy,
    And must see generations yet unborn.
    The whiskers of the great Leopard shall be oiled daily
    And kept tidy and neat. He who is rude to the Leopard
    Shall be devoured by the Leopard. *[Drums.]*

*[Exit OBON OBINI, followed by the crowd, amid traditional
    music. As the music sound recedes into the distance, KATAI
    starts to untie KENWENG, weeping angrily.]*

KATAI: See what can befall men who are out for change.
    See what ordeal men go through simply because they
    Are fighting for a brighter future for all.
    Because they are struggling to cleanse the land
    Of corruption and exploitation and injustice.
    So we have to live like underdogs
    In order to avoid torments? No way!
    The struggle continues. Sokoro, like others
    Before him, has gone. Gone to mobilise the spirits of
     war.
    The fight continues. Our children must not
    See these ugly days. *[Sound of thunder.]* Strike! Strike!

Strike this awful land! Strike all those who stand
In the way of progress. Strike even me,
If I, too, am involved. The land needs new inhabitants
And new ways. *[Helps KENWENG up, picks up the rope
used in tying him, looks at it furiously and throws it away with
a sigh.]*
Truly,
We are in slavery. Of the worst kind.
Deprived of fundamental human rights
Under our very roofs, condemned slaves
In our very land of birth.

KENWENG *[In a weak voice.]*: Take me home,
Take me home, before I bleed myself white.
Before I give up without seeing my son and wife again.

[Thunder.]

KATAI: Fight the battle, fight! Strike hard!
[Thunder again, this time louder. He trembles.]
The gods are angry;
Our ancestors are very offended.
The Earth is about to throw up the innocent blood
She was forced to drink. There shall be a terrible flood!
*[He supports KENWENG who is making an effort to
walk.]* No hesitation. We need to hurry out of here.
Oh, my God! You can't even walk?
See how a Leopard has been reduced to a cripple.
How long are we going to live
Under this canopy of savage cruelty? *[KENWENG
collapses. KATAI raises an alarm; he is restless. He starts
running from one point to another.]*
Who is there? Sokoro! Oh, that name! That name

again!
Where are you? I need help! Kenweng is dying,
Dying, too, to leave me alone? Who else do I have left
To join me in the freedom-fight? Help! Someone, help!
*[Enter OBON OBINI, OSERE, AKPARIKA and the six
GUARDS. KATAI stops abruptly and stands still; he is so
frightened and confused.]*

What now? Have you come back to take
The last heads? Da Sokoro is gone;
Kenweng is soon following.
See how he wriggles on the ground
Like a worm bathed in a strange potion.
His strength has deserted him;
He is dying, dying to leave me alone.
No one here has some human sympathy?
Will someone not make at least an effort to help?
Remember this is a man who has brought pride
And dignity to this clan. This is a man who has fought
Countless battles to secure our forest for us.
Must he be the one to receive this sort of humiliation?
Can this clan afford to lose a man of his calibre?

OBON OBINI *[In a frightened tone.]:* Akparika,
Take him away at once. Get some water boiled.
His body needs massaging. He must not die.

*[AKPARIKA and four GUARDS take KENWENG away.
KATAI bursts into tears, then stops and wipes his eyes.]*

OSERE *[To KATAI.]:* The Leopard too has
A heart of pity. Obon Obini has thought
It wise to come and talk to you.

KATAI [*Tearfully.*]: Our clan is sinking,
  The ground is breaking fast.

OSERE: Hold it down; let the King speak.

[*A long pause.*]

OBON OBINI [*Still frightened.*]: I heard a voice speak to
  me.
  From the world beyond it seemed to come.
  No. A clear voice from within me,
  Perhaps from around me. It spoke to me,
  Warning me…. [*He breaks off suddenly, stares blankly into
  space and collapses gradually with the fading of lights. After a
  while, dim lights take us to a scene where he faces three
  BAKANI for trial. Signal of Bekundi, the highest Traditional
  Society in the clan. This is best produced with the shell of a
  tortoise: "Ku ku ka ku ka ka. Ku ku ka ku ka ka. Ku ka
  ka ku. Ka ku ka ku ka. Ku ku ku ka ka ku. Ku ku ku
  ka. Ku ku ka. Ku ku ka." Ululation. Then communication
  between BAKANI and OBON OBINI; this takes the form
  of a mime. Clad in white garments, and each bearing an ancient
  looking traditional weapon, BAKANI are obviously
  admonishing OBON OBINI. OBON OBINI struggles in
  vain to get out of mire in which he is trapped. He begs
  BAKANI to have mercy on him but they are hesitant to forgive.
  After a while one of them moves forward and pulls him out, and
  the three exit in haste. Immediately, OBON OBINI takes a
  deep breath and looks up in supplication. Sudden fadeout; and
  shortly after lights take us back to the former scene where we
  now see OBON OBINI struggling to free himself from the
  supporting hands of OSERE and KATAI. He gives a sudden
  long scream.*]

Tra-a-a-a-apped!

[Enter AKPARIKA and the four GUARDS who immediately assist in holding down OBON OBINI.]

OSERE: Hold him firmly. *[Loudly.]* Firmly, gentlemen.

[Suddenly OBON OBINI causes the men to almost stagger to a fall. The GUARDS manage to find their feet, hold him down and help him sit up properly.]

OBON OBINI *[Panting heavily.]*: Trapped.
Trapped. Trapped in the swamps.

AKPARIKA: What is he saying?
OSERE: Leave him alone.

[OBON OBINI continues panting and gradually starts to regain consciousness. Perfect silence.]

OBON OBINI *[In a weak, gasping voice.]*: I'm sorry
For the terrible past.
I got trapped in the swamps.
Now I know I need to listen.
The problem had been I had no one
Who could bring me to reason.
All my men, how they fear me!
They give me honour due to a god.

VOICE *[Offstage.]*: Because they know
What they get from you, those sycophants.

OBON OBINI *[Still half conscious.]*: And they do me

71

Wrong by that. *[To KATAI.]* But it's not too late, my
son,
It's time we reasoned together. I shall on Saturday
invite
You and everyone to my palace.

AKPARIKA *[TO OBON OBINI.]*: What happened,
Your Highness?

OSERE: Leave him alone, I say.

VOICE *[Loudly, offstage.]*: The clan breathes
The breath of hope.

[Terrifying silence.]

OBON OBINI *[Looking around.]*: Who spoke?

OSERE *[Trembling.]*: Your Highness,
It was a strange voice that I heard.

OBON OBINI: And what did it say?

OSERE: That the clan breathes the breath of hope.

OBON OBINI: The clan breathes the breath of hope.
A new dawn comes, time for some reforms.
Now I know we need some change.

KATAI *[Happily.]*: Thanks be to the gods!
The spirits of our ancestors be praised!

OSERE: The tree of woe has touched the ground:

A new dawn comes with radiant rays.

OBON OBINI [*More conscious.*]: What do you mean
    By that kind of talk, Osere?
    You certainly are one of the treacherous snakes
    That crawl about in my palace.
[*In a mummuring tone.*] Humans are wicked creatures.
[*Struggling to get up.*] Come on, my son,
    Let me embrace you. [*Slumps back onto the ready*
hands of the GUARDS.] Your courage and your wits do
    speak
    The language of the gods. [*KATAI stands still,*
spellbound.] Come, come, come, my son.
    Let us make a sign of peace.
    Did you not hear that thunder blast
        soon after I left?
    There was a clear warning voice in it.

AKPARIKA [*Emotionally.*]: I fear for you, your Highness,
    I fear for you. It's hard to guess what strange illness
    Has taken possession of your head.

OBON OBINI: What?
AKPARIKA: But, my Lord.
OSERE: Stop! You can't speak when the Leopard roars.

AKPARIKA [*Summoning some more courage.*]:
    The roaring is gone. The present behaviour
    Of His Most Royal Highness is a thing to question.

OBON OBINI: Go on and speak; tell me more.
    And since you find me unfit, at this juncture,
    To be your king [*Showing his head.*], take off the crown.

73

AKPARIKA: No, my Lord, we can't come to that.

OBON OBINI: Why not? [*Manages to stand up alone, staggering a little bit.*] It's all yours now. [*Holding out the royal staff.*] Here, too, take it.

AKPARIKA [*Pleadingly.*]: No, my Lord,
That the gods forbid.

OBON OBINI: No way! Even my regalia I will
Surrender to you.

AKPARIKA: My Lord, please! That would mean a curse.

OBON OBINI: Now, listen! Have no fear.
The crown fits your head most squarely.
The gods be your guide!

AKPARIKA: Don't you bring down a curse on me, my Lord,
I've meant you no wrong.

OBON OBINI: But I am too insane to rule.

AKPARIKA: No one said you are insane, my Lord.

OBON OBINI [*Gains more strength, flaring up.*]:
But you just said it! Or am I deaf too? [...]
You are one of the treacherous snakes that lurk in
My palace. Pretending to be a worm.
Your stomach grumbles though your mouth
Seems sealed. Today is the day of true revelation.
Obini shall live with enemies no more!

AKPARIKA: My Lord, please! Forgive me.

OSERE: Tolerance, your Highness, tolerance!
    The King is father both of the young and old.
    [To AKPARIKA.] Get out of here, you drunk.
    [Exit AKPARIKA in haste.] I can't count how many times
        I've warned him to drink with sense.
    [As OBON OBINI paces back and forth in obvious anger.]
    The King is equal to the burden on his head.
    The gods know who to choose as King.

*[OBON OBINI goes on pacing, talking but not audible enough to
    be understood. A distant crack of thunder. A pause, then the
    sound of an ominous bird.]*

OBON OBINI: When ominous birds raise those
    sorrowful cries
    And the sky puts on an unsightly mask,
    A wise traveller takes precautions as he journeys on.

VOICE *[Offstage.]*: And peace shall reign in that Kingdom
    Where the King listens to the yearning of his subjects.
    The King himself shall wear a new and lasting crown.

OBON OBINI: The voice again!

OSERE: I heard it too.

OBON OBINI: So distinct, so exact
    And so full of good tidings.

OSERE *[In supplication.]*: May the Sun of Hope
    Shine on our land. *[To KATAI.]* My son, you see,

Our King is kind. You are born a blessed man.
Thank your god that you are free.

KATAI [*Thoughtfully.*]: Can this be true?
Can it be true [...] that Obini,
The one whose name even the elephant trembles
When it's mentioned, save in praise,
Can it be true that he has forgiven me?
What benevolent god must have knocked open
The rocky door of his callused heart?
[*A pause. Aloud.*] Or am I caught in a dreamland
Of wonderful occurrences
That have no substance and no reality?

OBON OBINI: Come on, my son, do not be amazed.
Your words did touch that part of me
Where my bed of reason laid buried
In mire of insane power. Now I rise above
The turbulent sea of that cruel obsession.
My Kingdom shall enjoy a new Sun
Whose beams shall leave no roof untouched. [*A pause.*]
Come, let me embrace you as sign that we are one,
As sign that we shall, from now henceforth,
Have an equal share of the bounty of our land.

OSERE: May our hearts be filled with peace!
May our ancestors prepare us a pool of blessings
For our daily bath! May our land enjoy
The warmth and peace of true leadership!
May the traits of brutality and bestiality
That characterise our present generation
Be drowned in the mighty ocean of love!

[A distant crack of thunder.]

OBON OBINI: Osere, I can see
    Your wisdom is charged with the power of love;
    I can see you are a man of peace,
    Though sometimes your tongue is vile.
    You have the blessings of our ancestors.
    Peace unto our land. Peace unto our children.
[To KATAI.] Peace unto you, my son.
    You are a young man of rare intelligence.
    I have you at my heart.
    Come let me embrace you
    For everlasting peace.

[OBON OBINI and KATAI embrace. Lights fade gradually to blackout, amid ululation and a deep sound of a huge wooden gong.]

[END OF PLAY]

Printed in the United States
By Bookmasters